Trait-Based Writing Skills

Grades 3 – 4

by Connie S. Martin

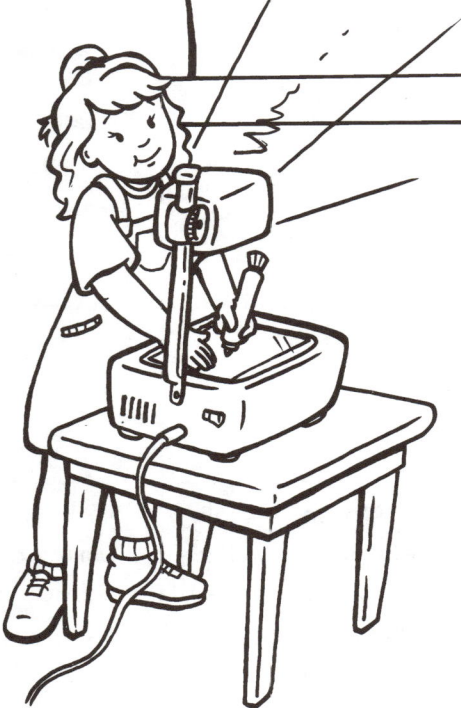

Activities Support These Learning Outcomes:
- Students will add important details to their writing.
- Students will apply organizational skills to their writing.
- Students will use interesting and precise language.
- Students will incorporate techniques, such as dialogue and varied sentence structure, to create flow.
- Students will understand the importance of audience.
- Students will improve mechanics.
- Students will learn to assess writing.

Carson-Dellosa Publishing Company, Inc.
Greensboro, North Carolina

Credits

Editors
Ashley Futrell
Kelly Gunzenhauser

Layout Design
Jon Nawrocik

Inside Illustrations
George Ling

Cover Design
Peggy Jackson

© 2005, Carson-Dellosa Publishing Company, Inc., Greensboro, North Carolina 27425. The purchase of this material entitles the buyer to reproduce worksheets and activities for classroom use only—not for commercial resale. Reproduction of these materials for an entire school or district is prohibited. No part of this book may be reproduced (except as noted above), stored in a retrieval system, or transmitted in any form or by any means (mechanically, electronically, recording, etc.) without the prior written consent of Carson-Dellosa Publishing Co., Inc.

Printed in the USA • All rights reserved.   ISBN 1-59441-066-6

Table of Contents

INTRODUCTION............................ 3	**SECTION 4: DOES MY WRITING FLOW?**........... 22
SECTION 1: WHAT DO I WANT TO WRITE?......... 4	Varied Sentence Beginnings.................. 24
Writing from Knowledge & Experience 6	Varied Sentence Length 25
Finding a Focus 7	Dialogue 26
Thinking It Through 8	Checking for Flow 27
Topic Sentence & Important Details............. 9	**SECTION 5: DOES MY WRITING SOUND LIKE ME?**.. 28
SECTION 2: DOES MY WRITING HAVE GOOD	Talking on Paper 30
STRUCTURE?............................. 10	Narrative Writing: Autobiographies 31
Interesting Introductions..................... 12	Persuasive Writing......................... 32
Story Elements 13	Report Writing 33
Sequential Transitions...................... 14	**SECTION 6: IS MY WRITING CORRECT?**......... 34
Satisfying Conclusions 15	Editing for Spelling........................ 36
SECTION 3: HAVE I PAINTED A CLEAR PICTURE?... 16	Editing for Capitalization.................... 37
Spicier Synonyms 18	Editing for Punctuation..................... 38
Using Homophones Correctly 19	Editing for Grammar 39
Descriptions 20	**ASSESSMENTS**............................. 40
Painting the Picture 21	Writing Rubric............................ 41
	Section Assessments....................... 43
	Answer Key .... inside back cover

Introduction

How many times have you carefully explained a writing assignment, only to look out at a sea of pitiful faces and blank stares? Some will wail mournfully, "I don't know what to write," while others will write about far too many topics at once. Students come to you with a variety of writing skills and varying levels of ability. How is it possible to accommodate each student? As a writing teacher, you can only accept students at their current levels and guide their growth.

The best way to serve as a writing guide is to model the thoughts and actions of a writer. In other words, teachers best teach writing by becoming writers. Show students how to think through the options for each aspect of a writing assignment, and they will feel more comfortable with the process and be empowered to become writers themselves.

If becoming a practicing, public writer for students sounds intimidating, remember that writing is simply telling something you want to share. Some students may be ready to share multipage stories. Others, especially second-language learners and very young children, may need to use a combination of drawing and writing to express an idea. Your goal is to teach writing skills while promoting an environment in which each child feels encouraged for all attempts at writing and respected when choosing to share that writing.

Trait-Based Writing Skills lessons provide grade-appropriate activities that require little planning or gathering of extra materials. Use them to teach and review trait-based writing skills, provide extra practice for individuals, or enhance any writing curriculum. Through these lessons, students will learn important trait-based language and methods and will also learn how to apply these skills to their own writing.

During the instruction portion of the lessons, model with the overhead projector or on chart paper to let students see your facial expressions as you verbalize thoughts and transfer those thoughts to writing. The reproducibles are sometimes incorporated within the teacher activities, but they are primarily designed for additional, independent practice of the lessons. Note that struggling writers at the third- and fourth-grade levels may need more modeling in order to understand and apply some concepts.

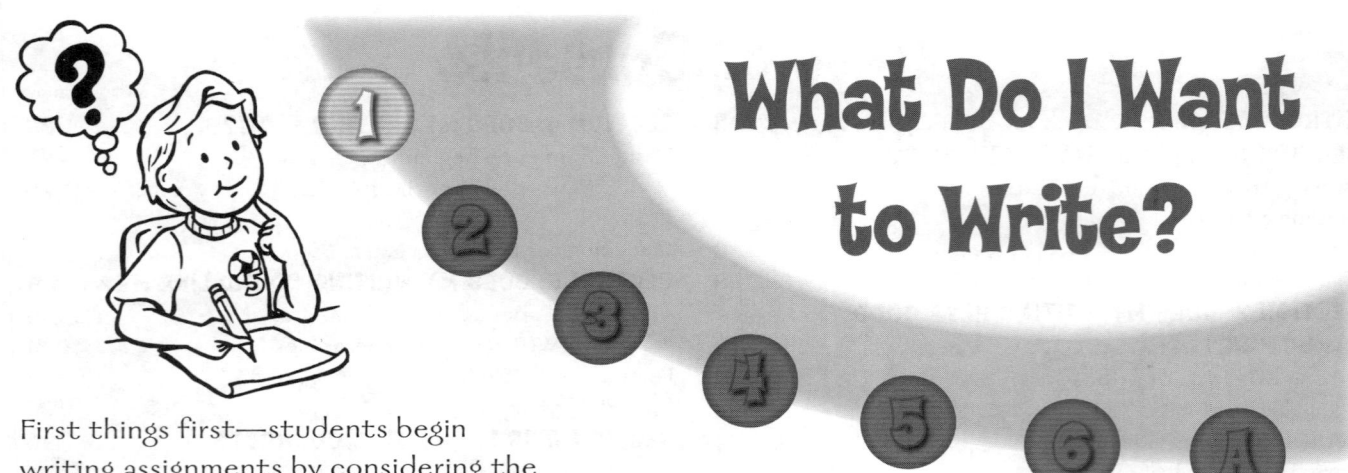

What Do I Want to Write?

First things first—students begin writing assignments by considering the topic. Wouldn't it be nice if they could always choose their writing topics? Students are always more motivated to write when the topics are relevant to their lives. It is not always possible to give them this freedom, but it is quite important to include opportunities for choice whenever possible. When a topic has been determined, a student must consider what to say and how to say it in an interesting manner. So, before the student puts pen to paper, there is much to be considered. Some students seem to complete this process naturally while others need to have it modeled for them. The following lessons will give students opportunities to practice these writing skills.

Writing from Knowledge & Experience

Write a variety of topics on individual slips of paper. Choose some topics that are familiar to students as well as some topics about which they would have little or no knowledge. Examples of potentially unfamiliar topics might include:

- How laser beams work
- How a television works
- How to cook a turkey
- How it rains
- Why the sky is blue
- History of the Panama Canal

Put the slips of paper in a bag and have each student draw a slip. Each student must write a paragraph about the topic even if it is unfamiliar to her. Tell students to guess about their topics if they are not familiar with the information. This will frustrate some, but reassure them that this is an activity to make a point. After writing, ask for volunteers to share their writing. Ask students what was easier: writing about something familiar or trying to write about something unfamiliar. Remind students to consider what they have to share about each topic when given a list from which to choose. This will help them select the best topic.

Finding a Focus

Tell students they have 15 minutes to write about anything they choose. When time is up, ask them how they chose their writing topics. Some students may say they thought about things (good or bad) currently happening in their lives. Others may say they thought about things they like to do. Remind students that it is easier and more fun to write about things that are familiar to them. With the class, brainstorm a list of relevant writing topics to display and refer to in the future. The list might include:

- My favorite person, place, or thing (food, movie, book, game, etc.)

What Do I Want to Write?

- The best (or worst) day ever
- Changes happening in my life
- Best friends
- How I learned to . . . (ride a bike, swim, ski, skateboard, cook, etc.)
- What I know about current events in my town, state, province, nation, or the world
- The time I was really . . . (scared, embarrassed, angry, upset, happy, etc.)
- Some things I know about . . . (snakes, astronauts, any special interest, etc.)

Remind students that topics should always be manageable and focused on important points they want to share with the reader.

Thinking It Through

When students are choosing their own topics, use the *Topic Organizer* (page 8) to help them organize their thoughts before writing. Make a transparency of the organizer or copy the information on the board. Model the organization process by telling students that you are trying to choose a writing topic. Verbalize your thought process as you consider and write down three possible writing topics. Analyze each topic aloud based on the criteria listed on the organizer. Choose a topic and brainstorm at least five details you could share with readers. Details do not have to be written in complete sentences—they can be listed in words and short reminder phrases for the brainstorming phase of the composition. However, if you prefer to emphasize good sentence structure at this stage, model the process of listing details using complete sentences.

Leave the completed model organizer on the board for reference. Give each student a blank copy of the organizer. Have students think about possible writing topics and complete their organizers on their own. Students may continue by writing the piece, or they may keep the organizers in their writing portfolios to use for reference when needed.

Topic Sentence & Important Details

Ask each student to bring in a short newspaper article that he finds interesting. You may want to bring in several newspapers and allow students to select their articles in class. As a model, share an article you have chosen. Ask students to listen for the topic sentence that tells what the article is about and for important details that are relevant to the topic. Have students raise their hands when they hear the topic sentence or an important detail. Discuss how to determine if some details are more important than others and why it is important to have various kinds of details. You may want to repeat this activity with more than one article to check for skill comprehension.

When you feel students have grasped the concepts of a good topic sentence and important supporting details, have them review the newspaper articles they chose. Ask students to underline the topic sentences and draw a circle around each important detail. Have students exchange articles to check that the topic sentences and important details were correctly identified. Discuss any disagreements. Let volunteers share their articles while the class listens for topic sentences and important details.

What Do I Want to Write? WRITING FROM KNOWLEDGE & EXPERIENCE

NAME _____

EXPERT ADVICE

Directions: Think of something that interests you. Make sure you know a lot about it. Maybe you play a sport, bake chocolate chip cookies, make beaded necklaces, or build tree forts. Maybe you know a lot about dinosaurs or famous artists. Fill in the blanks below and then write about your topic. Share interesting bits of information you think the reader will want to know. Use additional paper if needed.

My topic is: _____

List at least four interesting details you think the reader will want to know.

1. _____
2. _____
3. _____
4. _____

_____
_____
_____
_____
_____
_____

EXTRA

Imagine that you have been chosen to write an advice column in a newspaper. What would the topic of your column be? On a separate piece of paper, write your first column of advice.

What Do I Want to Write?

FINDING A FOCUS

NAME _____

ALL ABOUT ME

Directions: Fill in the blanks to tell about people and things in your life and why they are important. Use additional paper if needed. Then, follow the directions at the bottom of the page.

1. The most important person in my life is _____

   because _____

2. I really like to _____

   because _____

3. I really don't like to _____

   because _____

4. I was so proud when _____

   because _____

5. I know a lot about _____

   because _____

6. I will always remember the time when _____

   because _____

7. I was so scared when _____

   because _____

Now, choose one of the topics above. Circle the number of your topic. Remember to choose a topic that will be interesting to readers because you have a lot of details to share about it. On a separate piece of paper, write at least one descriptive paragraph about your topic.

CD-104037 • Trait-Based Writing Skills 3–4   © Carson-Dellosa

What Do I Want to Write?

THINKING IT THROUGH

NAME _____

TOPIC ORGANIZER

Directions: Fill in the organizer below to help you choose your own writing topic. First, list three possible writing topics and answer the three questions after each one.

1. Possible topic: _____
   Do you know a lot about this topic? ○ Yes ○ No
   Can you think of at least five details to share about this topic? ○ Yes ○ No
   Is this topic manageable? ○ Yes ○ No

2. Possible topic: _____
   Do you know a lot about this topic? ○ Yes ○ No
   Can you think of at least five details to share about this topic? ○ Yes ○ No
   Is this topic manageable? ○ Yes ○ No

3. Possible topic: _____
   Do you know a lot about this topic? ○ Yes ○ No
   Can you think of at least five details to share about this topic? ○ Yes ○ No
   Is this topic manageable? ○ Yes ○ No

4. Which one of your writing topics answers "Yes" to all three of the questions? That is your topic. Write it in the space below.

My writing topic is: _____

List at least five details you want to share about this topic.

1. _____

2. _____

3. _____

4. _____

5. _____

6. Other details I want to share: _____
_____

What Do I Want to Write?

TOPIC SENTENCE & IMPORTANT DETAILS

NAME _____

EXTRA! EXTRA!

Directions: Read the article and then follow the directions at the bottom of the page.

    If you want to know what's happening around you, read a newspaper. Newspapers carry information about important events in your town, your state, your country, and the world. There is so much information in a newspaper that it is divided into sections.

    The front section usually carries news about the most important things that happen in the world, whether they take place in your town or in another country. Maybe a new mayor was elected in your town, or maybe there was a huge fire at an old warehouse. Perhaps representatives from several nations met at the United Nations and signed a peace agreement that will affect all of the countries in the world.

    There's also the sports section. Usually, you can find news of local athletes and teams, as well as the scores of national and local teams in a wide variety of sports.

    Most newspapers also have a section for comics, a section for business, and a classified section for people who are trying to sell things or look for jobs. So, now you see why I said that if you want to know what's happening, you should read a newspaper. It has everything!

1. The topic of the article is: _____

2. Draw a star above the topic sentence.

3. List three important details you learned from the article. _____

   _____

   _____

   _____

4. Underline the sentences that give important details about the topic.

5. List three sections of a newspaper. _____

   _____

   _____

Does My Writing Have Good Structure?

A topic has been chosen, and a focus has been found. The student has thoughtfully considered important details to share. But, the information must now be written in a logical, orderly fashion if the reader is to understand what the writer is trying to convey. In order to attract readers' interest and attention, the writer must tempt the audience into wanting to know more and then provide just the right amount of information to satisfy readers' questions. The following lessons will give students opportunities to practice creating interesting introductions, using the elements of a good story, providing information in an appropriate order, and completing their writing with satisfying conclusions.

Interesting Introductions

Collect a selection of books with enticing introductions. Some books you may want to consider are:

- *Howliday Inn* by James Howe (Avon Books, Inc., 1982)
- *The Sign of the Beaver* by Elizabeth George Speare (Bantam Doubleday Dell Books for Young Readers, 1983)
- *Summer of the Monkeys* by Wilson Rawls (Bantam Books, 1992)
- *The Wall* by Eve Bunting (Clarion Books, 1990)
- *Mrs. Katz and Tush* by Patricia Polacco (Bantam Books, 1992)
- *The Three Questions* by Jon J. Muth (Scholastic Press, 2002)

Read a few introductions aloud to students. For some books, the introduction may only be the first sentence or two. In other cases, you may need to read the first paragraph, the first page, or even the first few pages. Discuss why introductions make readers want to continue reading the stories. Now, divide students into small groups. Have each student take out a book from the media center or from the classroom library and share the introduction with others in the group. When everyone has shared, have the groups discuss each selection and rank the introductions from worst to best. Ask each group to choose a representative to read their best introduction to the class. Discuss what makes each introduction enticing. Remind students to try to include interesting introductions when they write in order to capture readers' attention.

Does My Writing Have Good Structure?

Story Elements

Sometimes students will be asked to write simply to entertain. They may choose to write completely fictional tales rather than writing from knowledge and experience. Often, a story will still be based somewhat on an author's knowledge and experiences—emotions, human nature, personal experiences, etc. Regardless of the origin of the tale, the elements of a good story (setting, characters, problem/situation, plot, and conclusion) should be evident. These elements should be obvious in the stories students read, as well. Use the *Story Organizer* (page 13) to review the parts of a good story. Make a transparency of the organizer or copy it onto a large chart. Choose a story students have recently read and work as a class to discuss it. Have students help you fill in the information as you complete the organizer. Give each student a blank copy of the organizer. Have students keep the copies in their writing portfolios to use as they prepare to write new stories.

Sequential Transitions

Sequential transitions are used to connect sentences or paragraphs in a logical or chronological sequence. To demonstrate how to use good sequential transitions, assign topics or allow students to choose topics from a current unit of study. Have each student formulate a topic sentence and list three informative details about the topic. Each detail will become the main idea of a short paragraph. When students have prepared their topics and details, list some transition words and phrases on the board. Some suggestions are: *at first, to begin with, first of all, in the beginning, next, then, after this, afterward, finally, at last, in the end, eventually,* and *in conclusion*. Discuss how the correct use of transitions will aid in the organization and flow of information and will help readers understand what the writer is sharing. Ask each student to write his informative piece of writing consisting of a topic sentence and three well-organized, transitional paragraphs.

Satisfying Conclusions

Share a selection of short books that contain a variety of endings. Choose one that has a circular ending, such as *Two Bad Ants* by Chris Van Allsburg (Houghton Mifflin, 1988), one with a surprise ending, such as *The Frog Prince* by Jon Scieszka (Puffin, 1994), and one with an emotional ending, such as *The Keeping Quilt* by Patricia Polacco (Simon and Schuster, 2001). Discuss the different kinds of endings. Explain that in a circular ending, the conclusion goes back to the beginning of the story—it ends in the same place or same way as it began. A surprise ending does the unexpected, and an emotional ending touches readers and affects the way they look at life.

Have students recall a favorite book or story and decide if the author uses one of these types of endings. Ask students to explain how they know when a book has a certain type of ending. Discuss when it is best to use each type. Remind students that effective writers think carefully about story endings and choose something other than *The End* or *They lived happily ever after* because they understand that the conclusion wraps up the story and gives them a last chance to convey what is being shared.

Does My Writing Have Good Structure?   INTERESTING INTRODUCTIONS

NAME _____

CAN YOU BELIEVE IT?

Directions: Read the following three topics. Write an engaging title and an interesting introductory paragraph for each topic. Use additional paper if needed. Remember, an interesting introduction might give readers a hint of the events to come, throw them right into the action, answer a question, or just surprise them in some way.

1. While hiking one day, you find a briefcase filled with . . .

   _____
   _____
   _____
   _____

2. You discover your newborn brother or sister can talk—but only to you!

   _____
   _____
   _____
   _____

3. There is an elephant in the swimming pool!

   _____
   _____
   _____
   _____

Does My Writing Have Good Structure? STORY ELEMENTS

NAME _____

STORY ORGANIZER

Directions: Fill in the organizer to help you plan before you write a new story. Use additional paper if needed. You can also use the organizer to analyze existing stories as you read them.

Setting:
1. Where does the story take place? _____

2. When does the story take place? _____

Main Characters: Name each main character. Tell important details about the characters, like how they look and what they do that is important in the story.

1. _____

2. _____

3. _____

Problem, Conflict, or Main Idea:
1. What is the main character's goal? In other words, what does the main character hope to accomplish by the end of the story? _____

2. Are there problems that get in the way? _____ If so, what are they? _____
_____

3. How are the problems solved? _____

Important Plot Events: List the most important story events in order.

1. _____

2. _____

3. _____

4. _____

Resolution or Conclusion: How does the story end, and how does it affect the main characters? _____
_____

Does My Writing Have Good Structure? ② SEQUENTIAL TRANSITIONS

NAME _____

FIRST, THEN, FINALLY

Directions: Read the story. Underline each transition word or phrase.

Moving to a new house can be exciting, but it can also be a big pain! First, you have to decide what to throw away and what to keep. You will probably find things under the bed or behind the furniture that you have been looking for forever!

Next, you have to pack the things you want to keep. Things that could be broken should be wrapped carefully in cloth or paper. You don't want to get to the new place and open a box to find your CD player broken into a million pieces!

After you pack, you have to load everything into the truck and take it to the new house. Finally, when you get to your new room, you have to create your space all over again to make the new room feel like home. At last, the move is over, and you can start losing things that won't be found again until the next move!

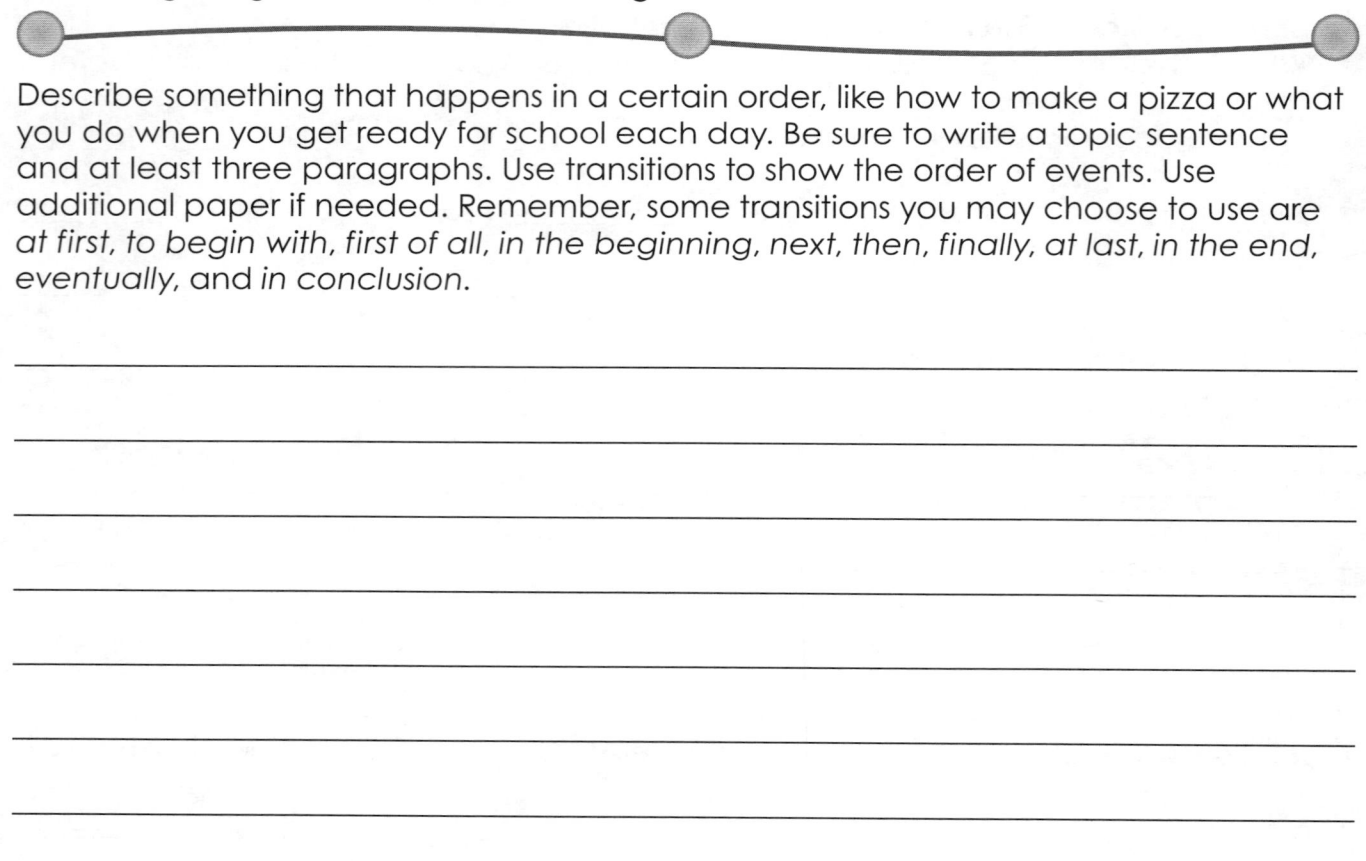

Describe something that happens in a certain order, like how to make a pizza or what you do when you get ready for school each day. Be sure to write a topic sentence and at least three paragraphs. Use transitions to show the order of events. Use additional paper if needed. Remember, some transitions you may choose to use are *at first, to begin with, first of all, in the beginning, next, then, finally, at last, in the end, eventually,* and *in conclusion.*

_____
_____
_____
_____
_____
_____
_____

Does My Writing Have Good Structure?   SATISFYING CONCLUSIONS

NAME _____

A BIG MISTAKE

Directions: Answer the questions. Then, read the story and write an ending for it. Decide if it should be a circular ending, a surprise ending, or an emotional ending. Use additional paper if needed.

1. What is a circular ending? _____

2. What is a surprise ending? _____

3. What is an emotional ending? _____

    I like old coins. I especially cherish an old gold coin my great-grandfather gave me for my birthday last year. He has had the coin since 1915, and he's sure it's worth a lot of money now. I usually keep it in a wooden box under my bed, but I took it to school yesterday to show my friends. That was one big mistake! Somehow, it fell out of my pocket. I retraced my steps to school, but I couldn't find it on the ground anywhere. Did it roll away? Did an animal take it? Did someone pick it up and spend it? Is it lost forever? I was just about to give up and slink home to confess my awful mistake to my mother, when suddenly . . .

_____
_____
_____
_____
_____
_____

EXTRA

On a separate piece of paper, write your own story beginning. Trade papers with a classmate and write the conclusion to his story while he writes one for your story.

Have I Painted a Clear Picture?

A writer's blank page is like an artist's clean canvas. An artist chooses colors for a painting in much the same way as a writer chooses words for a piece of writing. Both try to clearly communicate thoughts, feelings, and ideas. In each case, the clearer the picture, the better the audience will understand the piece. Student writers need the chance to practice finding just the right words to paint clear pictures in readers' minds.

Spicier Synonyms

Obtain four copies of a student thesaurus. Prepare a list of words for students to find in the thesaurus. Choose overused, general words, such as *big*, *bad*, *look*, or *said*. Write the first word at the beginning of a line on a large chart. Divide the class into four teams and give each team a thesaurus. At your signal, the first student in each team must search for the word in a thesaurus. The first student who finds the word and raises her hand to be recognized wins a point for her team. Have the student read the synonyms for the chosen word. Let the class choose three favorite synonyms. List the chosen synonyms beside the original word on the chart. Continue with all of the words on your list, allowing each team member to have a turn looking up a word. Display the chart for students to reference during writing. Remind students that they can often find more descriptive words to help clarify the pictures they are trying to paint in readers' minds.

Using Homophones Correctly

Play a matching game. Write each word from a set of homophones on separate index cards. Create enough cards for each student to receive one. Distribute the cards randomly. Remind students that homophones are words that are pronounced the same but are spelled differently and have different meanings. In their writing, it is important for students to use words correctly to paint the correct pictures in readers' minds.

Have students mingle without talking and find the student(s) holding the matching homophone word (or words). Then, give each student a sentence strip. Let groups of students work together to write a sentence for each word, leaving a blank where the homophone goes. For example, if the homophones are *right* and *write*, students might compose these sentences: *I gave the ____ answer. I will ____ a letter to my grandmother.* Collect the sentence strips. Put a set in a pocket chart. Have the class guess the missing homophones and tell how each should be spelled.

Have I Painted a Clear Picture?

Examples of homophones:
- blew/blue
- for/four
- sea/see
- hole/whole
- principal/principle
- meat/meet
- board/bored
- hear/here
- vain/vane/vein
- knot/not
- forth/fourth
- knew/new
- its/it's
- flour/flower
- rain/rein
- ate/eight
- plain/plane
- peak/peek
- wait/weight
- to/too/two
- heard/herd
- your/you're
- know/no
- weak/week
- pail/pale
- pain/pane
- mail/male
- eye/I
- wood/would
- threw/through
- their/there/they're
- peace/piece
- pair/pare/pear
- sail/sale
- main/mane
- bare/bear

Descriptions

Borrow or create amazing items for students to describe when writing. Choose items that will grab the senses! Examples might include an old, stinky sweat sock; a crystal bowl full of bright, colorful jelly beans; an interesting art print borrowed from the art teacher; an animal skull from the science lab; or anything else you can think of. Divide students into small groups. Make sure you have one more item to describe than the number of groups—for example, if you have six groups, you will need seven items. Number each item. Have a general discussion about writing descriptions. Remind students that comments such as *It is pretty* or *It is yucky* are not very descriptive. Students need to consider the five senses when they are looking for good descriptive words. Tell students that each group will secretly be given one item to describe. Whisper the item number to each member in each group. Give students time to quietly discuss their items. Have each group choose a recorder to compile a list of descriptive words and phrases suggested by group members. Collect all of the descriptions, read each one, and let the class guess which description fits which item. For a challenge, choose very similar items so that students will need to be extremely detailed in their descriptions.

Painting the Picture

Ask students to think about the picture that comes to mind when you say the following sentence: *The garbage was full of yucky stuff.* Discuss student responses. Note the different images created because the language in the sentence is too general. *Garbage* can mean many things, and what exactly is *stuff*? Now ask students to listen to a poem and think about the exact mind picture the words create. Read "Sarah Cynthia Sylvia Stout Would Not Take the Garbage Out" from *Where the Sidewalk Ends* by Shel Silverstein (HarperCollins, 1974). Discuss the images that are created when specific words are used.

Now, write a general sentence on the board, such as *I bought some great things at the mall.* Have students discuss the possibilities. What do *great* and *things* really tell the reader? What mind pictures are created? Ask students to rewrite the sentence using specific words to tell what *great things* they might buy at the mall. Remind students to choose specific words to create the exact mind pictures they want the reader to "see." Ask students to share some of their specific, descriptive items aloud.

Have I Painted a Clear Picture?   SPICIER SYNONYMS

NAME _____

A BETTER WAY TO SAY IT

Directions: Read each word. Write at least three synonyms for each word. Use a thesaurus to check your work if needed.

1. bad _____
2. good _____
3. said _____
4. cry _____
5. hit _____
6. wet _____
7. laugh _____
8. cold _____
9. hot _____
10. take _____
11. get _____
12. nice _____
13. pretty _____
14. little _____
15. big _____
16. pull _____

EXTRA

On a separate piece of paper, write at least three antonyms for each word. Remember, an antonym is the opposite of a synonym. For example: *hot* and *cold* are antonyms.

© Carson-Dellosa   18   CD-104037 • Trait-Based Writing Skills 3-4

Have I Painted a Clear Picture?

USING HOMOPHONES CORRECTLY

NAME _____

SURVIVING THE STORM

Directions: Read the story. Find 13 incorrect homophones. Circle each incorrect homophone and write the correct homophone above the circled word.

One Saturday afternoon, I left my house and headed off for a leisurely picnic in the park. Not long after I spread my blanket under a big oak tree, the clouds started to roll in. It was then that I new the storm was coming to ruin my picnic. I could here the thunder in the distance and smell the rein. It wasn't long before the wind began to blow and the rain started to poor. I could sea the lightning in the distance. I hid in an old barn. It was empty except for the sounds of birds rustling in the rafters. I guess they were hiding from the storm, too! Cobwebs were everywhere. Obviously, no won had used the barn in a long time, except maybe the sparrows and spiders. As I weighted for the storm to pass, I herd the raindrops splattering on the tin roof. Threw the window, I saw the trees swaying under the force of the howling wind. After a while, the storm finally blue over. I walked outside and saw the damage it had done. A peace of fence had been torn away, and sum tree limbs had been blown down. I was lucky to have found that old barn just in time! I was lucky I was safe. I was just plane lucky.

EXTRA

Can you think of some homophones? Try to think of five sets of homophones and write sentences with each word. For example: *I like to eat pears. I need two new pairs of socks.*

Have I Painted a Clear Picture? DESCRIPTIONS

NAME _____

USING YOUR SENSES

Directions: Think about each item. Using your five senses, think of and write at least three specific words or phrases to describe each item. Think about how the item looks, smells, sounds, tastes, and feels. Use additional paper if needed.

1. cheeseburger _____
_____

2. tarantula _____
_____

3. snowman _____
_____

4. porcupine _____
_____

5. milkshake _____
_____

6. mud _____
_____

7. roller coaster _____
_____

8. spaghetti _____
_____

EXTRA
Think of three items. On a separate piece of paper, write at least three descriptive words or phrases for each item. Trade papers with a friend and see if you can guess each other's items by reading only the descriptions.

Have I Painted a Clear Picture?

PAINTING THE PICTURE

NAME _____

SENSATIONAL SENTENCES

Directions: Read each general sentence. Rewrite each sentence using specific words to paint a picture in readers' minds. In some cases, you may need to write more than one sentence to paint an exact picture. Use additional paper if needed.

1. I had a great day! _____
_____

2. We saw lots of animals at the zoo. _____
_____

3. That monster costume looked really scary. _____
_____

4. I felt sick when I woke up this morning. _____
_____

5. I like sports. _____
_____

6. My favorite activity is cool. _____
_____

7. It is hard work doing my chores. _____
_____

8. I really don't like to eat yucky food. _____
_____

EXTRA

Choose one of the descriptions you wrote. On a separate piece of paper, add more sentences to make it into an introductory paragraph for a new story.

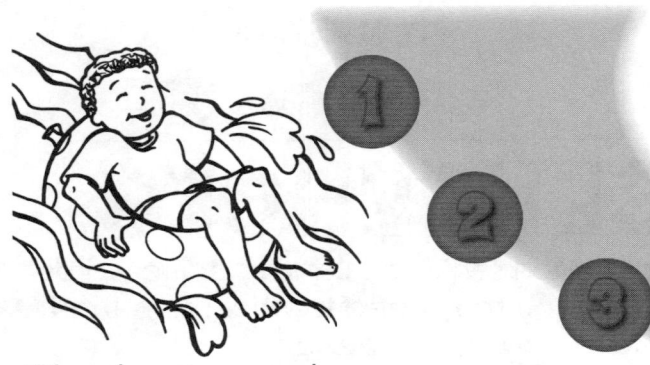

Does My Writing Flow?

What does it mean when you say something "flows?" While it can be difficult to define "flow," it is often easier to describe it. Flow is the quality that makes a beautiful piece of music pleasant to the ear. It is the characteristic that makes a poem roll off the tongue. It is what makes writing easy to read aloud, readily understood, and a pleasure to hear. Writing flows when it includes sentences that are crafted with a variety of beginnings to prevent monotony. They vary in structure—some are compound or complex while others are short and sweet. Dialogue, if present, seems real—readers can imagine the conversation actually taking place. The writer has crafted the piece so well that readers or listeners become immersed in the message the writing conveys.

Varied Sentence Beginnings

Write the following sentence on the board: *Tom met an old, ragged woman in the park last Saturday.* Ask students to suggest alternative arrangements for the words to create different sentence beginnings. (Examples: *While in the park last Saturday, Tom met an old, ragged woman. Last Saturday, Tom met an old, ragged woman in the park.*)
Now, write the following sentence parts on the board:
won the competition   the swimmers   last Friday   because of great teamwork
Have students rearrange the sections, using correct capitalization and punctuation, to create a variety of sentences with the same meaning. Let them share the variations. Remind students to consider the ways a sentence can be written to add variety and retain interest. Note, there are occasions when a writer will use sentences that have the same beginning to create an effect. While most third and fourth graders have not reached this level in their writing, it is important to recognize and discuss the effect when you encounter it during a lesson.

Varied Sentence Length

Review the difference between simple, compound, and complex sentences.
- ✐ A simple sentence contains a subject and verb, and it expresses a complete thought. It can contain compound subjects or verbs, and it does not have to be short. (Short: *Fire burns.* Long: *Fire crackles and burns brightly against the darkness of the night sky at the campground.*)
- ✐ A compound sentence contains two or more simple sentences connected by commas and conjunctions like *and*, *but*, and *or*. (*The fire burns brightly, and it keeps us warm.*)
- ✐ A complex sentence contains one simple sentence and at least one subordinate, or dependent, clause. It may or may not have a comma. (Comma: *As the fire burned brightly, we sang camp songs.* No Comma: *We slept soundly under the stars while the crickets chirped nearby.*)

Does My Writing Flow?

Choose a paragraph from a current reading lesson. Have students determine the number of simple, compound, and complex sentences in the paragraph. Have them note the various lengths of the simple sentences. Short sentences make a point, and longer sentences provide more detail or description. The best writing contains a variety of sentence lengths and structures. Just as with sentence beginnings, there are times when a writer uses sentences that are alike in length and structure to create an effect. Again, most third and fourth graders have not reached this level in their writing, but it is important to explain the effect when you encounter it in a lesson. Remind students that good writers consider what is to be said and the best way to say it in order to keep readers interested and to paint the right pictures in readers' minds.

Dialogue

Collect pictures to distribute or ask students to bring in magazine pictures showing people who could be having a conversation. Have students write two- or three-sentence summaries of what they imagine is happening in the pictures. Ask for volunteers to share their pictures and summaries. Next, review what students have learned about the correct placement of quotation marks and other punctuation when writing dialogue. Also, remind them to use descriptive synonyms in place of the word *said*. Now, have students write dialogue for the conversations that could be occurring in their pictures. Ask for volunteers to read their writing aloud. Remind the class that including dialogue in the right places can enhance a piece of writing.

Checking for Flow

One of the best ways to expose students to writing that flows is to let them hear it again and again. Choral reading provides students with this opportunity. In choral reading, students must concentrate on a piece of writing, noting when to start reading aloud and when to stop. They must consider proper tone and inflection. Even older students can enjoy choral reading if a subject is interesting to them. Poetry lends itself well to choral reading because the words of most poems flow easily. Choose a favorite poem or select one from the list below and have students practice choral reading. Assign lines or sections in a variety of ways. Some poetry options include:

- Poems from *Goops and How to Be Them* by Gelett Burgess (Goops Unlimited, 1998)
- "Jimmy Jet and His TV Set" from *Where the Sidewalk Ends* (HarperCollins, 1974) or other poems by Shel Silverstein
- "Eletelephony" by Laura E. Richards or other poems in *Favorite Poems, Old and New* selected by Helen Ferris (Doubleday, 1957)

When students are able to recognize the characteristics of writing that flows, they can begin to include the characteristics in their own writing.

Now, have each student use the *Writing Flow Checklist* (page 27) to review and revise a piece of writing from her writing portfolio. Discuss each item on the checklist and give an example of each. Have students check their own writing and then conference with you to determine specific revisions. When you are comfortable with each student's ability to check his own writing, you may choose to have students meet in pairs to check each other's writing and make revision suggestions.

Does My Writing Flow?   VARIED SENTENCE BEGINNINGS

NAME _____

GO TEAM, GO!

Directions: Read each sentence. Rewrite each sentence by rearranging the words, but do not change the meaning of the sentence. Remember to use commas if needed.

1. Gary went to the football game last weekend with Juan and Jeremy.

2. Since it was supposed to rain, the boys brought an umbrella.

3. The boys were lucky because it turned out to be a sunny day.

4. They bought hot dogs at the concession stand before the game.

5. The Raiders scored two touchdowns in the first quarter.

6. The quarterback threw a touchdown pass as the crowd cheered!

7. By the end of the game, the Raiders were winning by 24 points!

8. As they walked home, the boys talked about the great team.

9. When they arrived at Gary's house, they decided to play football in the yard.

10. Juan scored a touchdown as Jeremy chased after him.

EXTRA

On a separate piece of paper, explain why it is important to use varied sentence beginnings in your writing.

Does My Writing Flow? VARIED SENTENCE LENGTH

NAME _____

WHAT A "CAT"ASTROPHE!

Directions: Read the selection. Are there too many short, choppy sentences? Do some sentences go on and on? Rewrite the selection to show a variety of sentence lengths. Write some simple sentences as well as some compound and complex sentences. Use additional paper if needed.

    Peggy decided to ride her bike. She put on her helmet. She started off down the sidewalk. The sun was shining in her eyes. It was hard to see. A cat ran into the road. Peggy did not see it at first. She tried to stop. She missed the cat. She fell off her bike onto the street. "Ouch!" she cried. Her arm hurt a lot. Just then, a woman stopped to help her. She called Peggy's mom. Peggy and her mom put the broken bike into the back of the car and went to the emergency room at the hospital and the doctor took an X-ray and told Peggy her arm was broken. The doctor put her arm in a cast and gave her medicine to help her feel better and told her to come back for a checkup in three weeks. Peggy went home. On the way, she saw the same cat curled into a ball sleeping on the neighbor's porch, unaware of all of the trouble it had caused.

Does My Writing Flow? DIALOGUE

NAME _____

CLEVER CONVERSATIONS

Directions: Read each situation. Imagine how a conversation between the characters would sound. Choose one situation and circle the number of your choice. Give each character in the situation a name and write a conversation that you think they might have. Remember to use quotation marks and correct punctuation for writing dialogue. Use additional paper if needed.

1. two neighbors playing a game of one-on-one basketball
2. the owner of a candy store selling candy to a 10-year-old girl
3. two pirates reaching for the same treasure chest
4. a brother and sister picking out new school supplies
5. a little boy whining to his mother for a new toy at the store
6. three friends watching a sporting event on television
7. two friends playing a video game
8. a father and daughter discussing a new bedtime schedule
9. a mother and son discussing household chores
10. a family planning a vacation

Does My Writing Flow? CHECKING FOR FLOW

NAME _____

WRITING FLOW CHECKLIST

Directions: Read a piece of your writing aloud to yourself, your teacher, or a classmate. Answer the questions and follow the directions to revise your writing and improve the flow by making it easier to read aloud and easier to understand. Put a checkmark in the blank beside each item when you complete it.

1. Have I used a variety of simple, compound, and complex sentences? ○ Yes ○ No

   _____ Underline short, choppy sentences.

   _____ Combine some of your short, choppy sentences to make better compound and complex sentences.

2. Do my sentences have varied beginnings? ○ Yes ○ No

   _____ Circle the first word in each sentence.

   _____ Change the beginnings of some sentences to add variety to your writing, but do not change the meanings of the sentences.

3. Does the dialogue sound right for the characters? ○ Yes ○ No

   _____ Highlight sentences that include dialogue.

   _____ Improve any sentences that don't sound right for the characters.

4. Have I used correct punctuation, especially for dialogue? ○ Yes ○ No

   _____ Place punctuation for a direct quotation inside the quotation marks.

5. Have I used a variety of synonyms for the word *said*? ○ Yes ○ No

   _____ Draw a box around the word *said* each time you have used it.

   _____ Think of a more descriptive word that fits the action, such as *cried*, *chatted*, or *wailed*, especially in dialogue.

6. Is my writing easy to read aloud? ○ Yes ○ No

   _____ Share your writing with a classmate or with your teacher.

   _____ Discuss changes and suggestions with your classmate or teacher.

7. Revise your writing on a separate piece of paper. Then, share the new version with a classmate or with your teacher.

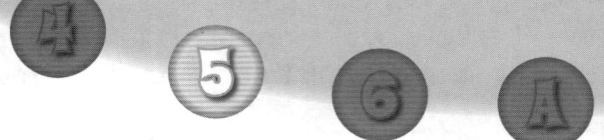

Does My Writing Sound Like Me?

There is a difference between classical music and rap and between Renaissance art and cubism. In each case, there is uniqueness. In writing, there is also uniqueness, that special "something" that lends personal perspective and expression to the writing. You can probably read a student's paper and identify the author simply because you have read many other papers by the same author, and you know that student's style. Developing that style is often difficult for students. They need to learn to relax and simply "talk on paper" as though holding a conversation with the reader. There are so many writing rules that it is easy to forget to encourage students to express themselves authentically. The type of expression depends on the purpose of the writing and the audience. The best way to help students begin to understand writing style is to share a variety of writings by different authors for different audiences. Some excellent books to share are:

- *If I Were in Charge of the World and Other Worries: Poems for Children and Their Parents* by Judith Viorst (Aladdin, 1984)
- *Where the Sidewalk Ends* by Shel Silverstein (HarperCollins, 1974)
- *John Henry* by Julius Lester (Puffin, 1999)
- *The True Story of the 3 Little Pigs!* by Jon Scieszka (Puffin, 1996)
- *The BFG* by Roald Dahl (Puffin, 1998)
- *Harriet the Spy* by Louise Fitzhugh (Yearling, 2001)

Talking on Paper

For centuries, people have kept diaries and journals to record the activities of daily life. They focused on conveying their thoughts and feelings by "talking on paper." Share excerpts from journals and diaries, such as:

- *Top-Secret, Personal Beeswax: A Journal by Junie B. (and Me!)* by Barbara Park (Random House Children's Books, 2003)
- *Castle Diary: The Journal of Tobias Burgess* by Richard Platt (Candlewick Press, 2003)
- *Dear America* series and *My America* series (Scholastic)

Discuss why diary and journal entries sound as though the writers are "talking on paper" as if having one-sided conversations with no one in particular. Discuss how the authors write about whatever is on their minds at the moment, noting their feelings and thoughts about events occurring around them, as well as recording vivid descriptions of places, people, and events. Ask students what they learn about each author from the contents of the entries. How old is each writer? Is it a boy or a girl? Where does the writer live? What is the time period? How are events affecting the author? Do students feel a connection with the writer? Remind students to try to "talk on paper" when

Does My Writing Sound Like Me?

they write in order to connect with their readers in the same way they have connected with the journal and diary authors.

Narrative Writing: Autobiographies

Remind students that a biography is the story of a person's life written by someone else. An autobiography is the story of a person's life written by that person. Famous, infamous, or unknown, everyone has a life story. Share excerpts from a few autobiographies, such as:

- *26 Fairmount Avenue* by Tomie dePaola (Putnam Publishing Group, 2001)
- *Thank You, Mr. Falker* by Patricia Polacco (Philomel, 1998)
- *Through My Eyes* by Ruby Bridges and Margo Lundell (Scholastic, 1999)
- books from the *Little House* series by Laura Ingalls Wilder

Send students to the media center to check out autobiographies of famous people or select a collection to display in the classroom. Have each student choose an autobiography to read at home or in class. After reading, have students select three events from their books to share with the class. Discuss how the writers include specific details and let their distinct personalities shine so that readers feel connected to them. Discuss how each person became famous. Ask students if and for what reason they think they might be famous some day.

Persuasive Writing

Ask students to think about all of the ways advertisers try to influence potential customers by persuading them to purchase certain products (contests and prizes on the backs of cereal boxes and in the tops of drink bottles, prizes in fast food meals, television advertising, complete lines of paraphernalia based on the newest movie characters, etc.). Bring an empty box of unhealthy children's cereal to class. With students, review the nutrition information for the cereal, as well as the items advertised on the back of the box. Have students consider the following questions:

- Do you like this cereal? Is this cereal good for you? Would you want this cereal if the advertised item(s) and prize(s) were not offered on the back of the box? Are you being influenced to buy this cereal because of the advertising? If the cereal does not offer a prize or item, would you buy it? Why or why not?

Lead students in a debate about the appropriateness of offering incentives on the backs of cereal boxes. Some may think it is acceptable, because consumers always have the option to buy or not to buy. Others may feel it is a way to sell an unhealthy product. Have students write persuasive letters to the manufacturer, stating their opinions. Have them explain reasons for their opinions and any actions they want to persuade the manufacturer to take (for example: keep offering prizes, but eliminate some of the sugar; make everyone a winner; etc.). Mail the letters. You may also want to see if the manufacturer has a Web site to which students could send persuasive E-mails.

Report Writing

Students sometimes feel that report writing is a dull recitation of facts. However, even in report writing, students can "talk on paper" and let their personalities shine. Distribute copies of the *Rainforest Animals* worksheet (page 33). Read the examples aloud. Have students underline the identical facts found in both reports and discuss which report is more interesting and why.

Does My Writing Sound Like Me? TALKING ON PAPER

NAME _____

YOU'LL NEVER BELIEVE IT!

Directions: Imagine you are keeping a journal or diary. Think of an important day that occurred recently. Pretend it is that day again. Write a diary or journal entry for that day and include your thoughts and feelings about things happening in your life, big or small. Try to "talk on paper." Use additional paper if needed.

_____
_____
_____
_____
_____
_____
_____
_____
_____
_____
_____
_____

EXTRA

Keep a diary or journal for one week. Use a favorite pen or cool paper. Staple the pages together to make a short diary or journal and design a cover for your book.

Does My Writing Sound Like Me?

NARRATIVE WRITING: AUTOBIOGRAPHIES

NAME _____

ALL ABOUT ME

Directions: Choose three important events in your life and list them on the time line. Then, choose one event and write about it as though it will be included in your autobiography when you are famous. Be sure to describe the event in great detail. Use additional paper if needed.

Event 1:   Event 2:   Event 3:

Let me tell you about the time in my life when . . .

_____
_____
_____
_____
_____
_____
_____
_____
_____

Does My Writing Sound Like Me?

PERSUASIVE WRITING

NAME _____

TAKING ISSUE

Directions: Consider the following four issues. Choose one of the issues or use the blank in number 5 to write in your own important issue. Circle the number of your choice. Write a letter to persuade someone to believe as you do and try to let your personality shine. Remember, there is no right or wrong answer for any of the questions. Be sure to state your opinion and explain at least three reasons for how you feel. Use additional paper if needed.

1. Do you think you have a fair bedtime? Why or why not?
2. Do you think school uniforms are a good idea? Why or why not?
3. Do you think children should have to do chores? Why or why not?
4. Do you think children should be able to eat cake and drink soda for breakfast every day? Why or why not?
5. Other issue that is important to you: _____

_____
_____
_____
_____
_____
_____
_____
_____
_____
_____

Does My Writing Sound Like Me?   REPORT WRITING

NAME _____

RAINFOREST ANIMALS

Directions: Read each example of a short, informational report. Then, follow the directions and answer the questions. Use additional paper if needed.

Example #1:
   Many animals live in the rainforest. The harpy eagle lives in the rainforest. It is the largest eagle in the world. It is 3.5 feet (1 m) tall. Howler monkeys also live in the rainforest. They swing from tree to tree by holding on to vines. Another animal, the three-toed sloth, lives in the rainforest, as well. The sloth sleeps upside down. The sloth is the slowest mammal in the world. It moves approximately six feet per minute in the trees and less than one foot per minute on the ground.

Example #2:
   You will not believe some of the animals that live in the rainforest! Have you ever heard of the harpy eagle? It is the largest eagle in the world. It is 3.5 feet (1 m) tall. That's taller than my little sister. The harpy eagle dives from the trees to capture its food. Sometimes, it even tries to catch a howler monkey. Howler monkeys are called "howlers" because they make a loud scream that can be heard three miles away. I bet that is a scary sound to hear at night! Howler monkeys travel through the forest by swinging from vine to vine, kind of like Tarzan. Another rainforest animal is the three-toed sloth. What a name and what a weird, mixed-up animal! It does everything upside down while hanging from a tree branch. It is the slowest mammal in the world. It is so slow it only moves about six feet per minute when it is in the trees. No wonder. I'm sure it is hard to move from tree to tree while hanging upside down!

1. Draw a line under the facts in each report.
2. Circle the beginning sentence in each report. Which one is more interesting? _____

   Why? _____

3. Highlight the sentences that show the author's opinions in Example #2.

4. Do you think the author let her personality shine in Example #1? _____

   Why or why not? _____

5. Do you think the author let his personality shine in Example #2? _____

   Why or why not? _____

6. Which report would you rather read? _____ Why? _____

Is My Writing Correct?

Students can often complete language arts worksheets for a specific skill, but they seldom automatically transfer their knowledge of grammar rules to their writing. Even if a piece of writing is well thought out, interesting, and presented in an appealing manner, it loses its readability if the conventions are incorrect. Students must consider the correct use of spelling, capitalization, punctuation, and grammar. Editing is probably the least favorite aspect of the writing process for most students. With practice, however, they can learn to look at their writing with a critical eye for conventions. Over time, the use of grammar and editing skills will become a natural part of a good writer's writing process.

Create an Editor's Checklist for students to reference. Introduce one skill at a time, adding to the checklist as the year progresses. Students may begin by editing their own writing and then advance to editing their peers' work as skills evolve.

Example of an Editor's Checklist

SYMBOL	EXPLANATION OF THE SYMBOL	EXAMPLE
≡	Capitalize a lowercase letter	marco is my friend.
/	Use a lowercase letter	Tomorrow is my Birthday.
⊙	Insert a period	Shelly has two cats⊙
∧	Insert punctuation mark	I feel great! How old are you?
◯	Spelling error	Please take my (piktur)

Editing for Spelling

Have a spelling bee. Create a grade-appropriate word list to distribute to students. Give them a few minutes to study the list and any words displayed throughout the classroom. Then, have students put away their lists while you cover the word displays. Ask students to stand at their desks. Give each student a chance to spell a word that you select from the list or from the displays. Students should sit if they misspell their words. The last student standing is the winner!

Is My Writing Correct?

Now, give each student three index cards. Have each child write *1* on his first card, *2* on his second card, and *3* on his third card. Select a vocabulary word students should know. Write the word three times in a row across the board, misspelling it twice. Have students hold up their cards that show the number of the correct spelling of the word. Continue with other words as time allows.

Editing for Capitalization

Review rules for capitalization that the class has learned, such as the need to capitalize:
- holidays
- titles of books
- personal titles
- greetings and closings of letters
- geographical place names
- special events
- names
- the first letter of the first word in a sentence
- the first letter of the first word in a quotation, when appropriate

Write example sentences with incorrect capitalization on sentence strips. Display a sentence for five seconds and allow students to study it. Have students point out the letter(s) that should be capitalized and explain why. Discuss any disagreements. Continue with other sentences as time allows. Introduce the Editor's Checklist symbol for capitalization for students to use when editing their writing.

Editing for Punctuation

Review punctuation rules that students have learned. Give each student a copy of the following example: *I saw a group of ducks running in the road there were cars coming fast around the corner a boy on a bicycle swerved before running into the cars he screeched to a halt as the cars stopped the ducks safely crossed the road.*

Read the example aloud with no punctuation. Give students time to read it again to themselves and add punctuation where they feel it is necessary. Choose volunteers to share different versions of the example. Have students consider the following questions: *Were cars going fast around the corner, or did the boy on the bike come around the corner? Did the boy swerve before running into the cars, or, before running into the cars, did the boy screech to a halt? Did he screech to a halt as the cars stopped, or did the ducks cross the road as the cars stopped?* Remind students to use punctuation correctly so that readers can understand the intent of the writing. Introduce the Editor's Checklist symbol for punctuation for students to use as they edit writing assignments.

Editing for Grammar

Have a contest. Review irregular plurals (*knife-knives, cherry-cherries, mouse-mice, deer-deer*, etc.), irregular verbs (*drink-drank, swim-swam, fly-flew*, etc.), and subject-verb agreement (*We see/sees the dogs.*). Divide the class into two teams. Have the first student on each team go to the board. Define the category (*Write the past tense of . . . , Write the plural of . . . ,* or *Choose the right tense to complete the following sentence . . .*). Give the word or sentence. Each student who writes the correct answer earns a point for her team. Continue with the next student from each team.

Is My Writing Correct?   EDITING FOR SPELLING

NAME _____

KNOCK-KNOCK!

Directions: Read the jokes. Use the Editor's Checklist symbol to mark each misspelled word. Write the correct spelling above each word. (Don't count the people's names!)

Example: Please take my (piktur). *picture*

Knock-knock.
Who's there?
Wanda.
Wanda who?
Wanda's the new movee start playeing?

Knock-knock.
Who's their?
Marcus.
Marcus who?
Marcus down to by four tikets.

Knock-nock.
Who's there?
Olive.
Olive who?
Olive us are waching the footbal game at my howse.

Knock-knock.
Whose there?
Kenya.
Kenya who?
Kenya teech me how to use this mashine?

Knock-knock.
Who's there?
Ester.
Ester who?
Ester if we can play softball durring resess.

Knock-knock.
Who's they're?
Shirley.
Shirley who?
Shirley you're going to buy that beutaful dress!

EXTRA

On a separate piece of paper, make up at least three knock-knock jokes of your own. Be sure to use correct spelling!

Is My Writing Correct?

EDITING FOR CAPITALIZATION

NAME _____

FAMILY VACATION

Directions: Read the paragraph. Use the Editor's Checklist symbol to show where uppercase letters are needed.

Example: i saw a puppy in the park.

Vacation, here we come! mom said we could take an exciting vacation next summer, but we have to begin planning now. We went to see mrs. wilson at the fantastic vacations travel agency. She gave us a lot of information about places we could go. I think a trip through colorado, arizona, and new mexico would be so much fun. We might choose to visit the grand canyon. It has camping and horseback riding. my friend, lewis, said you can even spend the night at the bottom of the canyon. We could also go rafting on the colorado river. Dad thinks it would be best to go in april or may before it gets too hot. Maybe we could go during spring break. I bet my teacher, mr. bishop, would let me make up any assignments that I miss while i'm on vacation. He always says, "the world is a classroom." I guess he means you can learn something new anywhere. Maybe I could keep a journal of my experiences. I could title it "great times at the grand canyon." I'm excited. I'm ready. Let's go!

EXTRA

On a separate piece of paper, write and draw a brochure for somewhere you would like to go on vacation. The place can be real or imaginary.

Is My Writing Correct?

EDITING FOR PUNCTUATION

NAME _____

HOLIDAY CELEBRATIONS

Directions: Read the sentences. Use the Editor's Checklist symbols to show where punctuation is needed. Then, write in the correct punctuation.

Example: Jeff, said Amy, do you like pizza? I do. It is great!

1. Today is December 23 2005. Christmas is coming in just two days

2. I want a skateboard a stereo a video game and a bike

3. We will visit my grandparents in Houston Texas

4. Do you visit family and friends during the holidays

5. Eddies family celebrates Hanukkah Theyre going to Chicago Illinois over the holidays That's where Eddies grandmother lives.

6. Earlier this week Eddie said My grandmother makes the best cookies ever!

7. Anna celebrates Kwanzaa She says its really a special time when her family is able to come together

8. Although its a really long trip some of her family members come to visit from London England

9. Eddie Anna and I celebrate the holidays in different ways How do you celebrate the holidays

10. We hope youll have a happy holiday season too

EXTRA

On a separate piece of paper, describe how you celebrate the holidays. Do you do anything special? Do you have a favorite holiday? Why is it your favorite?

Is My Writing Correct?

EDITING FOR GRAMMAR

NAME _____

BAZAAR BARGAINS

Directions: Read the paragraph. Underline any words that are not grammatically correct. Write the correct word above the underlined word. Remember to look for incorrect subject-verb agreement, irregular plural nouns, and irregular verbs.

Example: The fall leaves in the yard <u>was</u> blowing in the breeze. *(were)*

There's an old junk shop down the street. Last Saturday, we seen lots of people going in and out, so we decided to take a look inside. There was boxs everywhere! On one table, there were a glass bowl full of plastic cherrys. Shelfs full of old books, dishs, pictures, and vases were along each wall. There were even a giant bowl of fancy old knifes, forks, and spoons. Some of them looked like they was from a faraway land! Maybe at one time they belonged to a sultan in the desert or a European princess. We talked to the owner, Mr. Roberts. He telled us he has owned the shop for 50 years! As we were talking, I looked to my right and saw a funny sight! There was a picture of a grinning little boy with three missing tooths perched on a nearby stack of newspapers. Suddenly, a clock in the corner began to chime. We realized we were going to be late for lunch, so we hurryed out of there fast! I knowed my mom would be pretty worried if we were late.

EXTRA

Have you ever been in a store that was filled with all kinds of goodies? What kind of store was it? What did you see there that was interesting, weird, creepy, or really cool? Write about the experience on a separate piece of paper.

CD-104037 • Trait-Based Writing Skills 3–4 © Carson-Dellosa

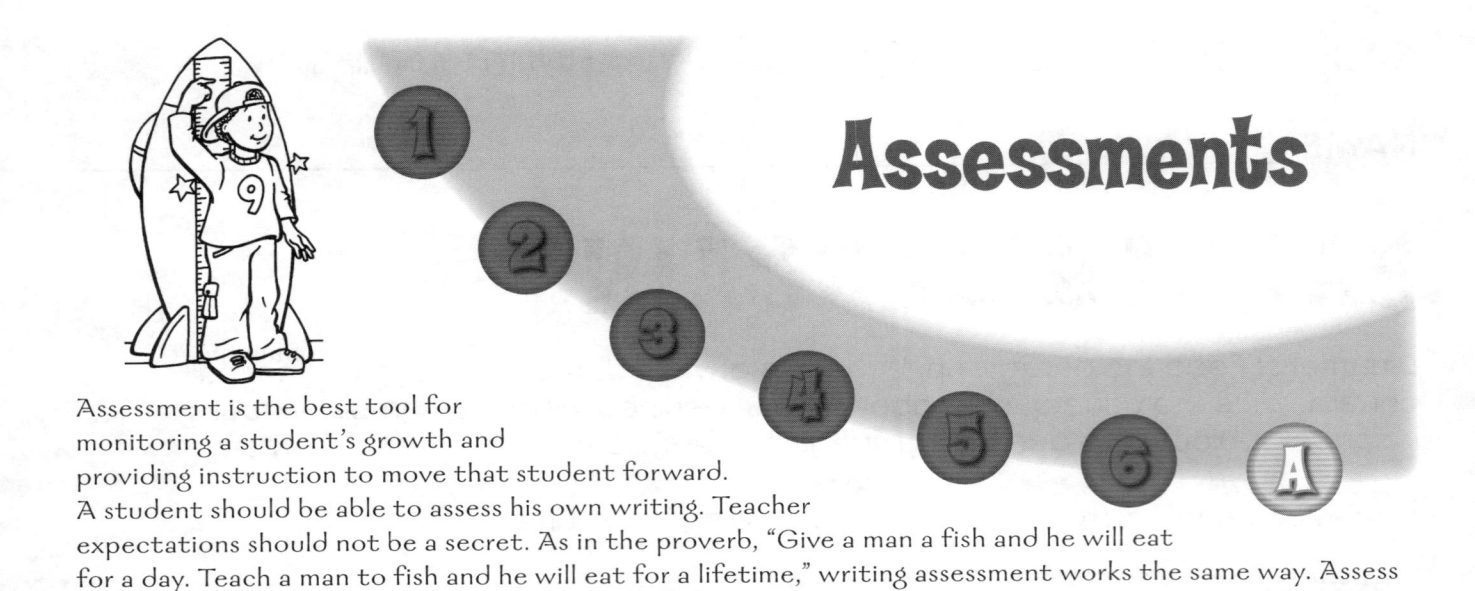

Assessments

Assessment is the best tool for monitoring a student's growth and providing instruction to move that student forward. A student should be able to assess his own writing. Teacher expectations should not be a secret. As in the proverb, "Give a man a fish and he will eat for a day. Teach a man to fish and he will eat for a lifetime," writing assessment works the same way. Assess a student's piece and he can correct that assignment. Teach him how to assess his own work, and he will have the tools to improve his writing skills.

Writing Rubric

Writing at higher grade levels becomes more complex. But, for writing at any level to be considered "good," it must have a focused topic, logically presented information, interesting vocabulary, well-constructed sentences, uniqueness, and correct mechanics. A writing rubric scale describes expectations and explains what effective writing looks like. Rubrics are divided into levels that describe the characteristics of writing a student should possess at that point. Students can use guidelines at each level to determine current strengths and identify weaknesses. It is your job to help students understand the rubric's language and to provide opportunities to practice assessing their own and others' writing.

Each student must also understand that her level on the rubric is not a judgment of her worth. It is a gauge of her current writing level that provides a framework for growth. When a student begins a piece, she might look over the rubric to remind herself of good writing characteristics, as well as your expectations for what should be included before an assignment is considered complete. Direct students who ask, "How many sentences/pages should I write?" to check the rubric, paying specific attention to areas for growth you have discussed. Using your guidance along with the rubric, students should be able to determine if they have met individualized expectations.

Struggling students may need to have the rubric translated into terms they can understand. You may want to put the information into a writing checklist and reserve the rubric for your teacher assessment. Begin the checklist with just a few items and add to it throughout the year as you introduce new skills.

Example of a Student Writing Checklist for Third and Fourth Graders

1. My name is on my paper, and my writing has an interesting title.
2. My topic is not too broad.
3. The introduction makes readers want to know more.
4. I have included details that describe and enhance my topic.
5. I have chosen words that paint a clear picture for readers.
6. My writing sounds like me.
7. The conclusion brings the writing to a close.
8. I have checked for correct spelling, capitalization, punctuation, and grammar.
9. I am ready to share my writing!

Putting an Exclamation Point on It

Each of the following assessment pages includes an extra challenge activity. Assign these activities to students who need more challenge and are ready to write independently.

Writing Rubric **A**

Section 1: What Do I Want to Write?	Section 2: Does My Writing Have Good Structure?	Section 3: Have I Painted a Clear Picture?
☐ **LEVEL 1** • No specific topic or main idea • Details are nonexistent or limited • Text is too short to develop topic ☐ **LEVEL 2** • Main idea exists, but is vague • Details do not relate to the topic • More information is needed ☐ **LEVEL 3** • Ideas are clear • Topic exists, but may be too broad to manage successfully • Limited details ☐ **LEVEL 4** • Ideas are clear • Topic is focused & manageable • Details relate to topic & provide adequate information ☐ **LEVEL 5** • Ideas are original & clear • Topic is focused & manageable • Supporting details grab readers' interest	☐ **LEVEL 1** • No sense of beginning, middle, & end • Disorganized • Lacks direction ☐ **LEVEL 2** • No clear introduction • Sequencing, if present, is not logical • No clear ending ☐ **LEVEL 3** • Introduction is present, but flat • Ending exists, but lacks closure • Organization is loose • Transitions are attempted ☐ **LEVEL 4** • Introduction catches readers' interest • Ending provides adequate closure • Clear organization • Transitions may be few, but are logical ☐ **LEVEL 5** • Fresh "hook" for the introduction • Ending provides closure, but also leaves readers wishing for more • Sequence is logical • Smooth transitions	☐ **LEVEL 1** • Limited vocabulary • Words used incorrectly • Lack of communication ☐ **LEVEL 2** • Simplistic language • Familiar words used repeatedly • Dull verbs ☐ **LEVEL 3** • Correct use of words • Varied word choices • Attempts to use colorful language ☐ **LEVEL 4** • Effective use of language • Specific word choices enhance interest • Conveys precise meaning ☐ **LEVEL 5** • Interesting, rich vocabulary • Strong verbs • Descriptive adjectives • Paints a vivid picture in readers' minds

Writing Rubric

Section 4: Does My Writing Flow?	Section 5: Does My Writing Sound Like Me?	Section 6: Is My Writing Correct?
☐ **LEVEL 1** ✎ Sentences begin the same way ✎ Run-on sentences ✎ Fragments ✎ Difficult to read aloud	☐ **LEVEL 1** ✎ No sense of audience or purpose ✎ Does not engage readers ✎ No sense of commitment to the writing	☐ **LEVEL 1** ✎ Misspelled words affect meaning & make writing difficult to read ✎ Punctuation generally missing or incorrect ✎ No obvious understanding of paragraphing ✎ Lack of correct grammar & usage
☐ **LEVEL 2** ✎ Sentences are correct, but short & choppy ✎ Lack of variety in sentence structure ✎ May be read aloud, but doesn't sound natural	☐ **LEVEL 2** ✎ Little sense of audience or purpose ✎ Occasional attempts to sound sincere by speaking directly to readers ✎ Writing seems flat	☐ **LEVEL 2** ✎ Many spelling errors ✎ Punctuation often missing or incorrect ✎ Limited paragraphing ✎ Frequent grammar & usage errors
☐ **LEVEL 3** ✎ Sentences generally correct, yet lack interest ✎ Some variety found in sentence patterns ✎ Writing sounds routine	☐ **LEVEL 3** ✎ Limited sense of audience & purpose ✎ Writer attempts to convey sincere feelings ✎ Writing sometimes sounds mechanical	☐ **LEVEL 3** ✎ Correct spelling of many common words ✎ Punctuation often correct ✎ Paragraphing usually correct ✎ Grammar & usage usually correct
☐ **LEVEL 4** ✎ Generally, sentences are well constructed ✎ Writing has flow & rhythm ✎ Easy to read aloud	☐ **LEVEL 4** ✎ Some sense of audience & purpose ✎ Expresses sincere, honest feelings & engages readers ✎ Shows some commitment to the writing	☐ **LEVEL 4** ✎ Few spelling errors ✎ Punctuation often correct ✎ Correct paragraphing ✎ Grammar & usage correct
☐ **LEVEL 5** ✎ Complete sentences begin in a variety of ways ✎ Variety of sentence patterns ✎ Writing has flow & rhythm ✎ Easy to read aloud	☐ **LEVEL 5** ✎ Writing is appropriate for audience & purpose ✎ Readers feel a connection to the writer ✎ Writing sounds natural ✎ Shows strong commitment to the writing	☐ **LEVEL 5** ✎ Occasional spelling errors ✎ No noticeable mistakes in punctuation ✎ Organized in paragraphs ✎ Grammar & usage make writing easy to read

Section 1: Assessment Ⓐ   WHAT DO I WANT TO WRITE?

NAME _____

I REALLY DON'T LIKE . . .

Directions: Choose one of the following topics or choose your own. Be sure you know a lot about the topic, and it is small enough to manage. Circle your choice.

1. your least favorite subject in school
2. your least favorite game to play
3. your least favorite chore to do
4. your least favorite food
5. your least favorite _____

List at least five details you want to share about your chosen topic.

1. _____
2. _____
3. _____
4. _____
5. _____

Write about your topic and include your five details. Use additional paper if needed.

_____
_____
_____
_____
_____

EXTRA

Now that you've written about something that is your least favorite, think of its opposite—your favorite! Write about it on a separate piece of paper.

CD-104037 • Trait-Based Writing Skills 3-4   © Carson-Dellosa

Section 2: Assessment   **A**   DOES MY WRITING HAVE GOOD STRUCTURE?

NAME _____

PARACHUTE PANIC

Directions: Read the story. Then, follow the directions and answer the questions.

    Man, oh, man! What a thrill! I can still feel it! You won't believe it, but I jumped out of an airplane today. No kidding! I went to a skydiving school in town. They let you skydive while strapped to one of their experts.

    First, I had to take a lesson on how to put on the equipment and how to hold on to Jordan, my instructor, while we were in the air. Next, I had to put on the flight suit and buckle up. Then, we boarded the smallest plane I've ever seen. My heart was really thumping. The plane went higher and higher. I thought about all kinds of things. What if the door opened, and I was too scared to jump? What if Jordan didn't really know what she was doing?

    Finally, the moment came. The plane was high enough. Jordan opened the door. The wind was whipping like crazy. I couldn't hear anything, so I just had to hold on and hope for the best. Jordan gave me a "thumbs up" sign and we dove out of the plane. We sailed through the air for what seemed like forever. I was terrified, happy, and amazed all at once. It was too much. I started feeling sick, so I just closed my eyes. Eventually, Jordan pulled the cord, and the parachute opened. We slowed down and drifted gently to the ground. I opened my eyes just as we landed. Whew! What a rush! I can't believe I jumped! But then, I was never really scared. Not one bit.

1. Write a tempting title for this story. _____

2. Draw a line under all of the sentences in the introduction.

3. Does the introduction make you want to read more? _____

   Why or why not? _____

_____

4. Circle each transition word.

5. On a separate piece of paper, rewrite the last paragraph to create a different conclusion for the story. You can make it silly or serious, but make it satisfying.

EXTRA

Have you ever dreamed of doing something really daring? What was it? What do you think it would be like? Write about it on a separate piece of paper.

Section 3: Assessment Ⓐ   HAVE I PAINTED A CLEAR PICTURE?

NAME _____

FIND THE PERFECT WORD

Directions: Read the instructions for each section and fill in the blanks.

Write at least three descriptive synonyms for each word.

1. good _____
2. cold _____
3. said _____
4. big _____
5. bad _____

Fill in each blank with the correct homophone.

6. (blew, blue) The ribbon on the gift is _____.
7. (blew, blue) The man _____ his trumpet.
8. (one, won) Our basketball team _____ the last three games.
9. (one, won) Please give each child just _____ cookie.
10. (hour, our) The doctor will see you in one _____.
11. (hour, our) Would you like to come to _____ house for dinner?
12. (sea, see) The three-masted ship sailed out to _____.
13. (sea, see) Did you _____ a movie last weekend?

EXTRA

Imagine you are asked to design a new amusement park ride. On a separate piece of paper, describe it using specific details so that the builders can get to work. Do not use general sentences like *It is big* or *It is fun*. Use specific words to paint pictures in readers' minds.

Section 4: Assessment   Ⓐ   **DOES MY WRITING FLOW?**

NAME _____

THE COWBOY SNOWMAN

Directions: Read the paragraph and then follow the directions.

It was cold. It was snowing. John went outside. Tom went outside. Rick went outside. They wanted to build a cowboy snowman. They rolled the snow. They made three snowballs. One snowball was big and one snowball was bigger and one snowball was the biggest of all. Rick asked Tom to get a hat for the snowman. Tom said he would get a cowboy hat from his dad. Rick asked John to find a scarf. John said he would borrow a bandana from his sister. They built a cowboy snowman and they hung a rope from one arm to lasso horses and they even put an old pair of cowboy boots at the bottom of the snowman so that he looked like he was wearing them. They looked at their snowman. They smiled. They named him Tex.

Rewrite the paragraph to make it easier to read. Use additional paper if needed. Include the following changes:
1. Change some of the sentence beginnings to add variety.
2. Combine some of the short, choppy sentences.
3. Make really long sentences into a few shorter sentences.
4. Add dialogue to show when someone is talking. Remember to use quotation marks and correct punctuation.

_____
_____
_____
_____
_____
_____

EXTRA

If you were building a snowman, how would you dress it? On a separate piece of paper, draw a picture and write a good description of your snowman.

Section 5: Assessment (A)   **DOES MY WRITING SOUND LIKE ME?**

NAME _____

AROUND THE WORLD

Directions: Imagine you are writing a letter to a new friend in another part of the world. Give the new friend a name. Think of where your friend lives and what life might be like there. Pretend this is your first letter to your new friend. Tell the friend things about your life and about yourself you want to share. Describe things that are important to you. Be sure to "talk on paper" to let your personality shine.

_____
_____
_____
_____
_____
_____
_____
_____
_____
_____
_____
_____
_____

EXTRA

Consider all of the things that are different for your friend who lives in another part of the world. What do you think you do that is different from the things your friend does? Write a letter describing these things to your friend and ask about the different ways of life in his faraway country.

Section 6: Assessment Ⓐ **IS MY WRITING CORRECT?**

NAME _____

LEARNING TO EDIT

Directions: Use the Editor's Checklist symbols to show where corrections need to be made for spelling, capitalization, and punctuation. Then, underline grammatically incorrect words. Remember to look for incorrect use of subject-verb agreement, irregular plural nouns, and irregular verbs. Above each incorrect word, write the correct form.

≡ capitalize a lowercase letter   ∧ insert punctuation mark

⊙ insert a period   ⬭ spelling error

    Editing a piece of righting is hard work. You has to edit for spelling capitalization punctuation and grammar. Sometimes its hard to spot words that arent spelled corectly Sometimes it's hard to know the write word to use. the best way to learn is through practice practice practice. Are your writing always correct the first time I bet it isn't. Most peoples have to make sum changes when they check there writing Nobody is perfekt after all! If you get most things right the first time, you are doing grate Congratulations to you But, you should never stop practising. The more you practices and studies your rules, the easier editing will become

    learning to edit is a lot like learning to do math. At first, it seems really hard to learn to add subtract multiplie and divide. however, after lots of practice and help from the teacher it get easier and eesier Editing is very similar, don't you think At the beginning, its really hard to remember all of the rules for spelling, capitalization, punctuashun, and grammar. But, in time, it start to get easier. thank goodness

EXTRA

On a separate piece of paper, write a conversation between two students about their favorite and least favorite school subjects. Describe what each student likes and dislikes and why. Remember to use correct punctuation for quotations.